Structural Wonders

Eiffel Tower

Bryan Pezzi

Published by Weigl Publishers Inc.
350 5th Avenue, Suite 3304, PMB 6G
New York, NY 10118-0069

Website: www.weigl.com

Library of Congress Cataloging-in-Publication Data

Pezzi, Bryan.
  Eiffel Tower / Bryan Pezzi.
      p. cm. -- (Structural wonders)
  Includes index.
  ISBN 978-1-59036-719-3 (hard cover : alk. paper) -- ISBN 978-1-59036-720-9 (soft cover :
alk. paper)
  1. Tour Eiffel (Paris, France)--Juvenile literature. 2. Paris (France)--Buildings, structures, etc.-
-Juvenile literature. I. Title.
  NA2930.P49 2008
  725'.970944361--dc22
                                        2007012111

Printed in the United States of America
  2 3 4 5 6 7 8 9 0 11 10 09 08

Photograph Credits
Every reasonable effort has been made to trace ownership and to obtain
permission to reprint copyright material. The publishers would be pleased
to have any errors or omissions brought to their attention so that they may
be corrected in subsequent printings.

All of the internet URLs given in the book were valid at the time of publication.
However, due to the dynamic nature of the Internet, some addresses may have
changed, or sites may have ceased to exist since publication. While the author
and publisher regret any inconvenience this may cause readers, no responsibility
for any such changes can be accepted by either the author or the publisher.

Project Coordinators: Heather C. Hudak, Heather Kissock
Design: Terry Paulhus

Contents

What is the Eiffel Tower?

Humans have been building structures since they could use tools. The techniques and materials have changed throughout the ages, but nearly all cultures take part in building structures. A structure is anything that is constructed from many parts. Houses, office buildings, churches, towers, and monuments are structures.

Some structures are known throughout the world. The Eiffel Tower is one such structure. It stands as a symbol of Paris, France. Located on the Champ de Mars near the Seine River, the tower is a massive structure. It was built for the Paris Centennial **Exposition** in 1889. During this time, the **Industrial Revolution** was changing how people lived and worked. The Eiffel Tower was an example of these changes. It was different from any structure built before. A better understanding of science allowed people to build in new ways. New materials and building techniques were used.

The Eiffel Tower was built by a French engineer named Gustave Eiffel. At 1,024 feet (312 meters) high, it was taller than any other structure at the time. The previous record holder, the Washington Monument, was only 555 feet (169 m). One of the reasons Eiffel's tower could reach such a great height was Eiffel's use of building materials. While the Washington Monument was made of heavy stone, the Eiffel Tower was built of iron. Metal was replacing wood and stone as a popular building material. It was strong and light, and it could be produced more cheaply. Parisians thought the large, metal Eiffel Tower looked unusual. Some thought it destroyed the city's beauty. Today, it is difficult to imagine Paris without this structure.

Quick Bites

- About 6 million people visit the Eiffel Tower every year.
- The first floor to the top of the Eiffel Tower receives a fresh coat of paint every five years. The entire tower is painted every 10 years. The Eiffel Tower has changed color six times since it was built.
- Today, the Eiffel Tower stands 1,063 feet (324 m) high. This is 39 feet (12 m) higher than when it was constructed. An antenna has been added to the top of the tower, increasing its height.

Building History

In the late 1800s, France went through a period known as the *Belle Epoque*, or the "beautiful era." After years of war and hardship, France was enjoying a time of peace and prosperity. The development of new industries and a growing empire had led to greater wealth for the French, and they wanted to show the world that France was a great power.

Gustave Eiffel included drawings of the Eiffel Tower in his book, *The 300-Meter Tower*.

The government planned a great exposition for 1889. Its purpose was to show the technological advances that France had made. The planners wanted to find a symbol for this event. They decided a great tower should be built on the Champ de Mars, a park in Paris. The structure was to be made of metal. The base would measure 410 square feet (125 square meters), and the tower would be 1,000 feet (305 m) high. The government held a contest to choose a design. More than 100 people submitted entries. Gustave Eiffel, a French engineer, was the winner. Eiffel was known for his innovative use of metal in bridges and other structures.

Construction of the tower began in January 1887. With only two years until the Paris Exposition, Eiffel had very little time. He and his assistants made thousands of drawings. Every part of the tower was sketched out.

The Eiffel Tower's foundations were built in 5 months. The metal pieces took 21 months to assemble.

June 1884: Eiffel's chief engineers, Emile Nouguier and Maurice Koechlin, present the initial design for a 1,000-foot (305-m) tower to Eiffel.

September 1884: Eiffel registers a patent for a metal structure that can exceed 1,000 feet (305 m).

May 1886: The French government announces a design competition for the 1889 Centennial Exposition. Gustave Eiffel is chosen as the winner.

January 1887: Excavation of the Eiffel Tower's proposed site begins.

June 1887: The Eiffel Tower's **foundation** is in place.

July 1, 1887: Construction begins on the Eiffel Tower.

March 1888: The first level is completed.

July 1888: The second level is completed.

March 31, 1889: The Eiffel Tower is completed, almost two months ahead of schedule.

May 6, 1889: The Paris Centennial Exposition opens.

Beginning in the mid-1800s, Universal Expositions were held every 11 years in Paris. In 1889, the exposition celebrated the 100-year anniversary of the French Revolution.

These plans ensured that not a bolt, **rivet**, or **girder** would be out of place. All the pieces were prepared in Eiffel's factory on the outskirts of Paris. In total, about 18,000 pieces were built. The pieces were transported to the construction site and assembled by workers.

The Eiffel Tower drew about 11,000 visitors each day of the festival.

Parisians watched as the tower was built. Not everyone liked the massive structure. A number of writers and artists banded together to protest. These critics thought Eiffel's tower was a giant example of bad taste. They did not believe the engineer had any idea of beauty or style. Despite the criticism, Eiffel's tower was built as planned and on schedule. It was completed in March 1889, about five weeks before the start of the exposition. The fair lasted for six months.

The Eiffel Tower was the focal point of the Paris Exposition.

Big Ideas

Gustave Eiffel knew that the use of metal would allow him to build bigger structures. He had used iron in his own designs for bridges and **viaducts**. Eiffel knew that the same kind of metalwork could be used in a monumental structure such as a very high tower.

In the United States, an engineering firm called Clarke, Reeves & Co. had proposed building a tower for America's Centennial. It would have columns of wrought iron connected by horizontal and diagonal beams. At 1,000 feet (305 m), it would be nearly twice the height of the Washington Monument. The project was not built due to lack of funds. Eiffel and his colleagues were inspired by the idea of this tower.

Emile Nouguier and Maurice Koechlin were engineers in Eiffel's company. They had been working on the idea of a tall tower for many years. Their plan was to have four large columns made up of metal girders. The columns would curve inward and join together at the top. Three platforms at different levels would allow visitors a spectacular view of the city. Eiffel also hired an architect named Stephen Sauvestre to work on the tower's appearance. Sauvestre planned the large arches that stretch between the legs of the tower. All of these design elements gave the tower its distinctive appearance.

Web Link:
To find out more about the Washington Monument , go to www.nps.gov/archive/wamo/home.htm

1) The end of the Paris Exposition of 1889 was marked by the blast of a cannon placed on one of the Eiffel Tower girders.
2) The Champ de Mars was the site of the Paris Exposition of 1889.
3) French aeronaut Eugene Godard took pictures of the exposition from a balloon.

Profile:
Alexandre-Gustave Eiffel

Alexandre-Gustave Eiffel was born in 1832 in Dijon, France. As a child, he showed an interest in science. He studied chemistry and graduated from the Ecole Centrale des Arts and Manufactures, one of Europe's top engineering schools. Eiffel then took a job with an engineering firm that specialized in steam engines and railroad equipment. When the company was taken over by a Belgian firm, Eiffel was named head of research. His first design was a 72-foot bridge made of iron.

At the age of 25, Eiffel began to work on major projects. His first big job was to oversee the construction of a bridge in Bordeaux. The 1,600-foot (488-m) iron bridge would cross the Garonne, one of the wildest rivers in France. As a timesaving measure, he developed a new method of pile driving. In this process, foundation materials, such as wood logs or steel posts, are pushed into soft ground using **hydraulic presses**. This technique was successful, and the bridge opened on time. Eiffel earned a reputation as an efficient builder who used innovative techniques.

Eiffel started his own business and opened metalworking shops northwest of Paris. Eiffel became known as the "magician of iron." He was especially interested in the use and appearance of **wrought iron**. Eiffel's technique of crisscrossing iron beams gave a webbed appearance. This was his trademark style.

THE WORK OF GUSTAVE EIFFEL

Garonne River Bridge, Bordeaux, France (1860)
Eiffel's first major project, the Garonne River Bridge, spans the Garonne River in Bordeaux. The 1,600-foot (488-m) bridge was constructed using a system of hydraulic presses to drive piles into the 80-foot- (24-m-) deep river.

Douro River Bridge, near Oporto, Portugal (1876)
The Douro River Bridge spanned the 525-foot- (160-m-) wide Douro River and was supported by a huge arch. A series of crisscrossed beams formed the arch. The two halves of the bridge were constructed separately and met 200 feet (61 m) above the middle of the river.

From 1867 to 1885, Eiffel's company built 42 railway bridges and viaducts. Some of these structures set records for the highest or longest bridges built. One of Eiffel's projects was the Statue of Liberty. The statue was a gift from France to the United States. French sculptor Frédéric-Auguste Bartholdi designed a plaster model. Eiffel used this model to plan and design an iron frame. The frame had steel beams that were attached to a granite base. Once the frame was complete, sheets of copper were attached. This technique resulted in a stronger, lighter structure that could withstand tremendous weight and natural forces. The completed statue was the largest ever built, at 151 feet (46 m) high. Once the statue was complete, it was taken apart. The pieces were then shipped to New York.

The Statue of Liberty, also designed by Eiffel, is located on Liberty Island in New York City.

However, it was the Eiffel Tower that became the highlight of his career. After it was built, Eiffel's name became known throughout Europe and the world. In 1887, Eiffel agreed to build the **locks** of the Panama Canal. The project failed because of a financial scandal. After this, Eiffel retired from his business. He spent the later years of his life doing scientific research in **meteorology**, **radiotelegraphy**, and **aerodynamics**.

Pest Station, Pest, Hungary (1877)
The Pest Station train station was one of the first examples of the Art Nouveau style in architecture. Art Nouveau is an elaborate style known for its decorative metal components.

Sioule Bridge, near Clermont-Ferrand, France (1869)
The Sioule Bridge bridge stood 262 feet (80 m) above the Sioule River in south-central France. It was one of the highest bridges in the world at the time.

Garabit Bridge, Garabit, France (1884)
The Garabit Bridge was similar to the Douro Bridge, but much larger. It stood 400 feet (122 m) above the Truyere River and was 1,850 feet (564 m) long. A great metal arch, spanning 541 feet (165 m), reached across the river. At completion, it was the highest arched bridge in the world.

The Science Behind the Building

Gustave Eiffel had a strong background in science. In order to build a structure like the Eiffel Tower, he needed to understand all the scientific principles at work.

The Properties of Iron

When the Industrial Revolution began in Europe, metal became widely used as a building material. As an engineer, Eiffel needed to know the characteristics of different metals. Wrought iron, **cast iron**, and steel were common. Of the three, wrought iron was the heaviest and was unlikely to buckle. It was easy to work with and strong enough to withstand the elements. Cast iron was weaker and more brittle than wrought iron or steel. At the time, steel was fairly new and expensive. It was lighter than iron, but not as strong. After considering the options, Eiffel chose to build his tower out of wrought iron. It was the most practical material because of its strength, flexibility, and durability. Wrought iron was also available at reasonable costs.

Gustave Eiffel used an open lattice of lightweight trusses in his design so that wind would blow through the Eiffel Tower.

The Properties of Arches

At the base of the Eiffel Tower, there are four large archways stretching between the legs of the tower. Arches have been used for centuries. They can span great distances and carry heavy weight. Arches are often used to support the upper parts of a structure. They are useful in structures such as domes, covered walkways, and bridges. An arch supports the weight of a building by converting the downward force of the weight into an outward force. In the Eiffel Tower, that means the arches help transfer the weight from the top of the tower to the four metal columns at the base.

Withstanding Wind

In building the world's tallest structure, Eiffel's biggest challenge was to make the tower able to withstand the force of wind. He designed the piers, or supports, of the tower to curve inward. Through mathematical calculations, Eiffel knew that this was the best shape to withstand wind pressure. He built the tower not as one large solid, but as a network of crisscrossed iron beams. There are large amounts of empty space between the beams, so wind can easily pass through. Eiffel's design ensures the tower can withstand even the strongest Paris winds.

Web Link:
To find out more about about iron and steel, go to http://science.howstuff works.com/iron.htm

Science and Technology

Building a structure requires planning, physical labor, and technology. The Eiffel Tower was unlike any other structure ever built. Eiffel needed to use the most advanced technology available to him.

Creeper Cranes

Cranes are useful in the construction of many structures. They are tall machines with long arms used for moving things. Cranes can lift metal beams, large tools, and other heavy objects. The Eiffel Tower was such a tall structure that the workers needed an efficient way to lift materials to the upper levels. Eiffel used a special kind of crane for this task. Creeper cranes were small steam-powered cranes. They were mounted onto sloping tracks that crept up the piers of the tower. Without creeper cranes, there would have been no way to move materials to such great heights. The 13-ton (11.8-tonne) cranes could pivot a full 360 degrees and move up the tracks as the tower's construction progressed.

Tower cranes are used to construct today's buildings. They can be as tall as 265 feet (81 m) and carry loads as heavy as 19.8 tons (18 tonnes).

Hydraulics

Many early machines, such as creeper cranes, were operated by steam power. At the time of the Eiffel Tower's construction, a new, more efficient technology was developing. Hydraulics is a system that powers many of the machines on today's construction sites, including bulldozers, backhoes, and forklifts. A hydraulics system uses two pistons in cylinders filled with an incompressible oil. This is oil that cannot be squeezed into a smaller space. The cylinders are connected by a pipe, which may be any length or shape. When force is applied to one of the pistons, the force is transmitted to the second piston through the oil in the pipe.

Hydraulic systems use liquid to transmit force, allowing hydraulic lifts to easily haul thousands of pounds.

The Eiffel Tower was one of the first structures to include passenger elevators.

The pistons move back and forth to power the machine. Eiffel used hydraulic jacks to position metal girders in the Eiffel Tower. These jacks could lift and lower the beams, so they could be adjusted within a fraction of an inch. In addition to these jacks, Eiffel used a system of hydraulic elevators throughout the tower.

Elevators

The Eiffel Tower has 1,665 steps between the ground level and the top of the tower. Eiffel decided on a system of elevators to move workers and visitors between the different levels. Elevators for the tower could not simply run straight up and down. They had to travel up the curved, angled legs of the structure. The elevators also needed enough power to lift large numbers of people and be in continual use. Steam powered elevators had been used as early as the 1860s. Eiffel decided on a more powerful kind of elevator that used hydraulic technology. He hired three different companies to install elevators in the tower. Two elevators ran between the ground floor and the first platform. One elevator took passengers from ground level to the second platform. Another traveled between the first and second platforms. Finally, one more elevator took visitors from the second platform to the top of the tower.

Quick Bites

- The Eiffel Tower received major renovations between 1980 and 1985. The tower was strengthened, and new elevators were installed.
- When the tower was first built, the elevator to the top level held 110 passengers, or a maximum of 8 tons (7 tonnes).

Computer-Aided Design

Architects are trained professionals who work with clients to design structures. Before anything is built, they make detailed drawings or models. These plans are important tools that help people visualize what the structure will look like. A blueprint is a detailed diagram that shows where all the parts of the structure will be placed. Walls, doors, windows, plumbing, electrical wiring, and other details are mapped out on the blueprint. Blueprints act as a guide for engineers and builders during construction.

For centuries, architects and builders worked without the aid of computers. Sketches and blueprints were drawn by hand. Highly skilled drafters would draw very technical designs. Today, this process is done using computers and sophisticated software programs. Architects use CAD, or computer-aided design, throughout the design process. Early CAD systems used computers to draft building plans. Today's computer programs can do much more. They can build three-dimensional models and computer simulations of how a building will look. They can also calculate the effects of different physical forces on the structure. Using CAD, today's architects can build more complex structures at lower cost and in less time.

Computer-aided design programs have been used since the 1960s.

Eye on Design

Computer-Aided Design and the Guggenheim Museum, Bilbao

The Guggenheim Museum in Bilbao, Spain, is made up of a series of interconnecting shapes.

Frank O. Gehry is an expert at using computer-aided design to create structures. One of the world's top architects, Gehry is known for designing museums, concert halls, and colleges. One of his most complex structures is the Guggenheim Museum in Bilbao, Spain. Completed in 1997, the Guggenheim is a massive structure of interconnected shapes. Computers were used to deal with the mathematical complexity of the design. Gehry used a program called CATIA, which had been developed to design fighter planes.

A miniature model was built to show the general shape and design of the museum. This was converted to digital information using CATIA. A series of points were plotted onscreen. This series of points roughly described the shape of the physical model. The computer program manipulated, cleaned up, and smoothed out the points to create an outline of the structure. This would represent the skeleton of the building. Shading was added to represent the titanium panels that would cover the steel skeleton. Finally, the computer program generated drawings that were used to build parts of the building at a steel shop.

MEASURING THE EIFFEL TOWER

Location

The Eiffel Tower is located on the Champ de Mars, on the left bank of the Seine River in Paris, France.

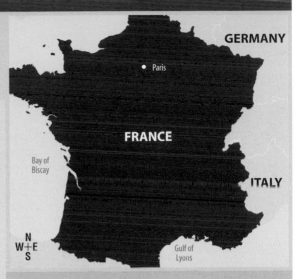

Height

- Height with antenna: 1,063 feet (324 m)
- Height of first level platform: 189 feet (57.6 m)
- Height of second level platform: 380 feet (115.7 m)
- Height of third level platform: 906 feet (276.1 m)

Area

The base of the Eiffel Tower is a square. Each side of the square is 410 feet (125 m) long. The area of the base is 2.5 acres (1 hectare).

Weight

The metal framework weighs 8,047 tons (7,300 tonnes).

The total weight of the structure is 11,023 tons (10,000 tonnes).

Other Interesting Facts

- About 55 tons (50 tonnes) of paint are required to paint the tower.
- About 230 million people have visited the Eiffel Tower.

Movement

The top of the structure sways up to 2.76 inches (7 cm) in high wind.

Environmental Viewpoint

Gustave Eiffel lived during the 1800s. This was a time when the Industrial Revolution was taking place in many countries. Iron and other mineral resources were mined for use in structures and machinery. At that time, people were not aware of environmental harm caused by mining. Today, we know that economic benefits of industry must be weighed against the environmental cost.

Iron, which was used to build the Eiffel Tower, must be mined from the earth. Iron ore is rock from which metal can be extracted. Most iron ore is obtained through open pit mining. To get at the ore, a large pit is dug in the ground. Natural **habitats** on the surface of the ground may be destroyed. The plants or animals that live there are lost. Environmental problems may include land erosion, sinkholes, and loss of **biodiversity**. More problems can arise when the iron ore is refined. The process of extracting metal from rock produces tailings, or industrial waste. If not properly dealt with, tailings can contaminate the land and water of the area.

Today, it is important for companies to have an environmental plan before mining an area. Data is gathered to better understand the **ecology** of the area. The company must do everything it can to reduce harm to the land, water, and air. When mining has ended, there must also be a plan for restoring the land to its former state. The pit is filled in, and habitat is restored to support plant and animal species again.

Numerous office and apartment buildings now neighbor the Eiffel Tower. The abundance of large, modern-day buildings has led to concerns worldwide regarding energy usage and its effect on the environment.

NERGY EFFICIENCY

The Eiffel Tower is a huge consumer of energy. It uses 7,000 megawatts every hour. Nine percent of this energy is used just for lighting. The Société d'exploitation de la Tour Eiffel (SETE), the company that operates the Eiffel Tower, is looking for ways to reduce the tower's impact on the environment.

On February 1, 2007, the Eiffel Tower took part in "Five Minutes of Rest for the Planet." This campaign was designed to raise awareness of energy consumption and global warming. On this evening, the tower turned off all its lights for five minutes. Only security lights were left on.

SETE has taken other steps in its everyday operations. The tower has a special "green contract" with its energy provider. This contract states that all energy must come from 100 percent renewable energy sources.

SETE has started replacing the tower's light bulbs with lower-energy bulbs. This action has helped reduce energy use by 30 percent. Other steps include a computerized system to control heating and lighting, and more efficient refrigeration systems.

Construction Careers

Eiffel's company employed more than 250 men to work on the tower. They were engineers, technicians, draftsmen, ironworkers, and construction workers. These jobs are still found in construction today.

Planning the tower required a team of 30 draftsmen. They produced thousands of detailed drawings for every part of the structure. Ironworkers made more than 18,000 pieces at Eiffel's factory just outside of Paris. The pieces were assembled with bolts and then shipped to the construction site. Eiffel's crew had to work long hours to meet the tight construction deadline. Through hard work and careful planning, the tower was completed on time.

Ironworkers

Ironworkers played a critical role in the construction of the Eiffel Tower. More than a century later, they are still needed to put up buildings, bridges, and other structures. Ironworkers read blueprints and install the metal parts of a structure. They set up the framework of a building and bolt the metal pieces into place. Sometimes, ironworkers are responsible for tasks such as welding or reinforcing concrete with metal bars.

They might also work on metal railings or stairwells. Ironworkers need to be in good physical condition. They must have good mechanical skills and be handy with tools. Ironworkers must always follow proper safety procedures to avoid injury on a construction site.

Tower Crane Operators

Cranes play an important part in the construction of any large structure. Eiffel used creeper cranes to crawl up the sloped sides of his tower. Today, tower cranes are common on construction sites. These are used to lift and move materials, machinery, and

heavy objects around the site. Tower crane operators need special training to use these large machines. They must work outdoors and at great heights. Usually, other workers guide the tower crane operator using hand signals or radio. Workers in this field need good balance, coordination, and the ability to judge distances.

Welders

Welders apply heat to melt and fuse metal pieces together. Working with heat and fire can be dangerous, so welders need to take special precautions. They must wear heavy gloves, long-sleeved jackets, and eye protection. Workers must be physically fit, have good coordination, and be able to focus on the job at hand. Some welders work in unusual places, such as extreme climates, under water, or even in outer space.

Glaziers

Glass is another building material that became popular in the 1800s. Today, glass is commonly used in homes, offices, and skyscrapers. Glaziers are people who install the glass parts in structures. Usually, glass is cut at a factory. It is then moved to a construction site where a glazier installs it. Glaziers use many tools, such as knives, suction cups, glass grinders, saws, and drills. The job may require lifting heavy glass panels or working at great heights. Glaziers must be careful to avoid injuries caused by broken glass.

Web Link:
To find out more about a career in welding, visit http://stats.bls.gov/oco/ocos226.htm

Notable Structures

The 1800s were a time of change for builders and architects. The Industrial Revolution allowed people to **mass-produce** new kinds of building materials, such as metal and glass. A new style of building emerged in Europe and the United States.

The Crystal Palace Exhibition Hall

Built: 1851

Location: London, England

Design: Sir Joseph Paxton, architect

Description: This giant hall was an intricate network of thin iron rods and sheets of clear glass. It was built as an exhibition space for London's Great Exhibition of 1851. The building's main body was 1,851 feet (564 m) long and 456 feet (139 m) wide.

Auditorium Theatre

Built: 1889

Location: Chicago, Illinois

Design: Louis Sullivan, architect; Dankmar Adler, engineer

Description: The Auditorium Theatre was the tallest building in Chicago at the time. It was built using modern technology, such as lighting and air conditioning. Today, the building is a National Historic Landmark. It has 24-karat, gold-leafed ceilings and detailed stencil patterns and murals throughout.

Structures could be very large and strong. At the same time, they could let in large amounts of light. The effect was a taller, lighter, and brighter space. The Eiffel Tower was only one of the many unique structures built in this style. There were many others as well.

Bon Marché

Built: 1876

Location: Paris, France

Design: Louis-Auguste Boileau, architect; Alexandre-Gustave Eiffel, engineer

Description: The Bon Marché was the world's first true department store. In 1876, the store moved into a new building. Engineered by Gustave Eiffel, the structure was built of iron and glass. Skylights in the ceiling allowed light to shine on interior courts.

St. Pancras Station

Built: 1868

Location: London, England

Design: William Henry Barlow, engineer

Description: St. Pancras is known as one of the great Victorian-era train stations. The building's train shed has an iron frame roof, which spans a distance of 243 feet (74 m). This huge enclosed space and the transparent iron framework looked futuristic to people of the nineteenth century.

Tall Buildings Through History

For centuries, people have strived to build the world's tallest structures. Prior to 1889, when the Eiffel Tower was built, there were no structures reaching more than 1,000 feet (305 m).

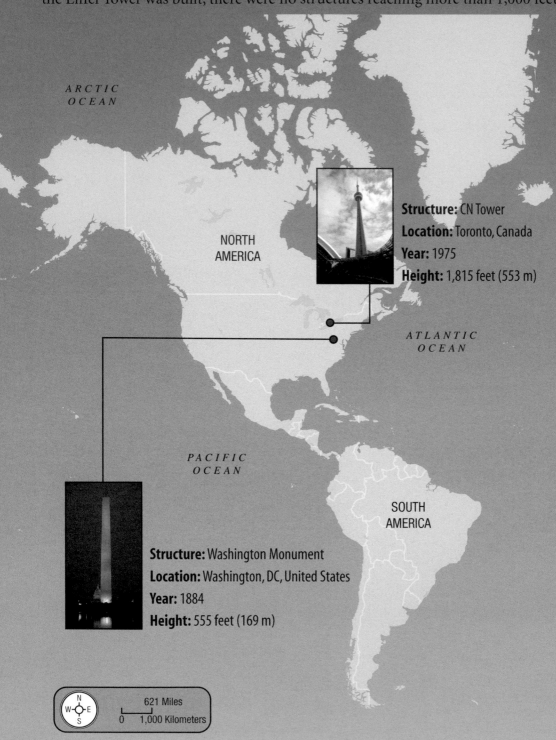

ARCTIC
OCEAN

NORTH
AMERICA

ATLANTIC
OCEAN

PACIFIC
OCEAN

SOUTH
AMERICA

Structure: CN Tower
Location: Toronto, Canada
Year: 1975
Height: 1,815 feet (553 m)

Structure: Washington Monument
Location: Washington, DC, United States
Year: 1884
Height: 555 feet (169 m)

N
W E
S

621 Miles
0   1,000 Kilometers

However, with better technology, these structures could rise higher. This map shows some of the world's highest structures throughout history.

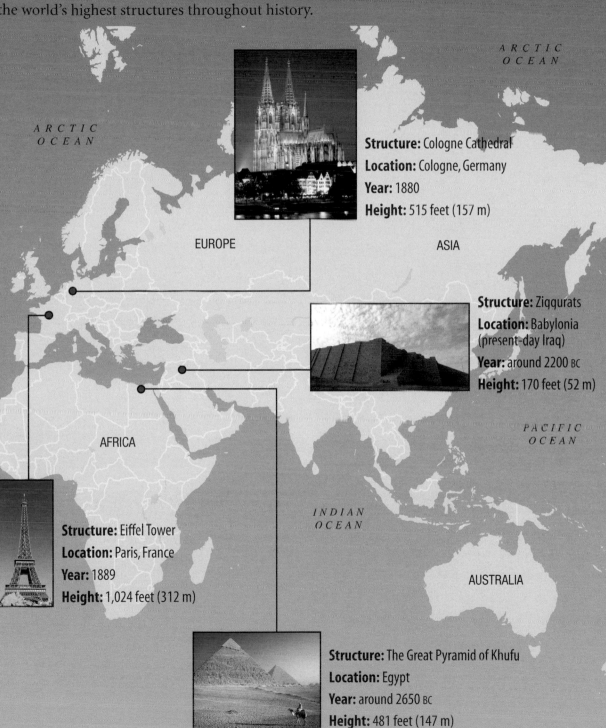

Structure: Cologne Cathedral
Location: Cologne, Germany
Year: 1880
Height: 515 feet (157 m)

Structure: Ziqqurats
Location: Babylonia (present-day Iraq)
Year: around 2200 BC
Height: 170 feet (52 m)

Structure: Eiffel Tower
Location: Paris, France
Year: 1889
Height: 1,024 feet (312 m)

Structure: The Great Pyramid of Khufu
Location: Egypt
Year: around 2650 BC
Height: 481 feet (147 m)

Quiz

Q What kind of metal was used to build the Eiffel Tower?

A The Eiffel Tower was made from wrought iron.

Q Where does iron come from?

A Iron is made from iron ore. Most iron ore comes from open pit mines.

Q Why are arches used in many large structures?

A Arches convert downward force to an outward force.

Q What is computer-aided design (CAD)?

A Computer-aided design is a system that lets architects draft structural designs by computer.

Create a Beam

Gustave Eiffel was an expert at building structures out of metal beams. A beam is a piece of material that resists bending. The shape of a beam can affect how strong it is. Using stiff paper or cardboard, create beams in different shapes, and test each beam to find out how strong it is.

Materials
- several sheets of light cardboard or stiff construction paper
- sticky tape
- two piles of books
- weights, such as standard metal weights, marbles, or weights made out of modeling clay

Instructions

1. Fold or bend the paper to create beams in different shapes. Use tape to hold the beams in shape. Try the following shapes.

A	B	C	D
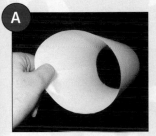	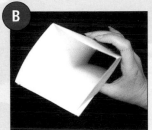	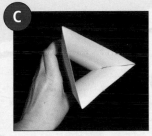	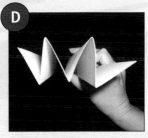
Bend one sheet of paper to create a hollow, circular beam. It will be cylindrical in shape.	Fold one sheet three times lengthwise, and then fold together to create a square beam.	Fold one sheet twice lengthwise, and then fold together to create a triangular beam.	Fold one sheet several times lengthwise to create an accordion-pattern beam.

2. Create two piles of books of equal height, with a gap between the two piles.

3. Bridge the gap between the book piles with a flat piece of paper first. Add weight to the paper until it collapses. Record how much weight was needed to collapse the paper.

4. Try each of the beams. Again, record how much weight can be added before the beam collapses. You might need to hang the weights underneath, depending on the shape of the beam.

5. Record data for each of the beams, and determine which of the beams could support the most weight.

Further Research

You can find more information on the Eiffel Tower, skyscrapers, and the world's tallest structures at your local library or on the Internet.

Websites

For more information about the Eiffel Tower,
visit the official site at www.tour-eiffel.fr/teiffel/uk/

To find out how hydraulic machines work, surf to
http://science.howstuffworks.com/hydraulic.htm

Learn more about elevators at
http://science.howstuffworks.com/elevator.htm

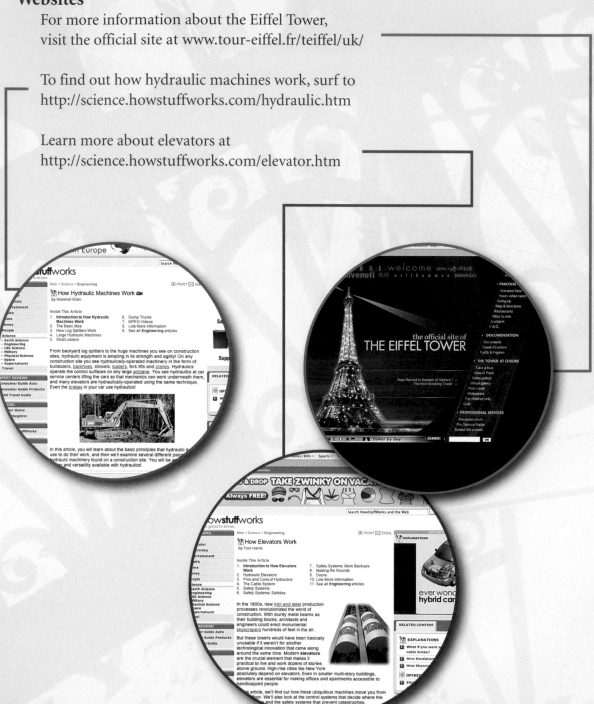

Glossary

aerodynamics: the study of how air moves around solid objects

biodiversity: the range of plants and animals in an environment

cast iron: iron containing so much carbon that it cannot be shaped by hammering, rolling, or pressing and must be poured into a mold to create a shape

ecology: a branch of science that concerns the relation of living organisms to their environment and to each other

excavation: the removal of soil and earth to make a hole in which a structure can be built

exposition: a public show or fair

foundation: a construction below the ground that distributes the load of a building or other structure

girder: a large iron or steel beam

habitats: natural homes or environments for living things

hydraulic presses: machines that use liquid pressure to enable a small force applied to a small piston to produce force on a larger piston

Industrial Revolution: a period in European history that was characterized by the development of industry on an extensive scale

locks: sections of a canal where the water level can be raised or lowered

mass-produce: to manufacture items to a standardized pattern in huge quantities

meteorology: the study of weather

radiotelegraphy: the science of transmitting and reproducing information by radio waves

rivet: a short metal pin or bolt that holds two pieces of metal together

viaducts: long, bridge-like structures that carry a road or railroad over a valley

wrought iron: a pure form of iron having low carbon content; often used for decorative work

Index